Let Me Teach You How To Pray Every Day

Angela Martin

Let Me Teach You How to Pray Every Day
ISBN: 978-1-946180-18-6
Copyright © 2019
Angela Martin
www.onederfulprayer.com

Published by:
Simpson Productions
www.SimpsonProductions.net

Contents

Dedication

This book is dedicated to my parents, Deacon Jimmie and Mother Elizabeth Martin.

During one of my weekly visits with them at their home, my mother said to me, "Where is your book? You need to write a book. That's the next step for you, write a book." I am so glad that she spoke those words to me. I actually conceived the idea for this book years ago, but she gave me the nudge that I needed to give birth to it. Her words resonated and followed me in such a way that left me with no other choice, I had to write this book. I am so grateful and thankful for my amazing parents. They are both my biological and spiritual parents. God gave me his best when he gave me them. So, here's your book Mama.

I also dedicate this book to my Onederwomen; the ladies who attend my monthly prayer meeting, *Onederful Prayer*. It is an honor and a privilege to serve you. I wouldn't have it any other way. My heart's desire and prayer to God, is that you will continue to grow, push, and press forward in prayer in order to receive God's highest and intended best for you.

A Note from Angela

ecause of my love for prayer and the platform that God has given me, people often ask me to help them increase their prayer lives. This is a question that I absolutely love to receive. Your interest in my book proves that you have this question in your heart as well, and that makes me very happy. I am overjoyed and so elated to give you the tools that you will need for your next level in prayer.

I will use a simple approach that will give you a plethora of benefits; if you will simply follow my lead. I designed this book to be an "easy read" that you can literally take anywhere. Once you have completed this book, you will want to share this message with others. So, please feel free to pass it on or bless someone with a copy of their own. You have no idea how much your life is getting ready to change. Are you ready? Let's go.

Introduction

*I*n the 1970's, pre-school and kindergarten were not mandatory to attend. Since I was the baby girl of seven children, my older siblings acted as my teachers. By the time I went to first grade, I was well advanced without the assistance of early-childhood education.

The seed of prayer was planted in me early as a child. My mother, Mother Elizabeth Martin, was one of the lead prayer intercessors at my foundational church, *New Friendship Missionary Baptist Church in Robbins, IL.* For the first six years of my life, I was always at my mother's side. She took me everywhere, including prayer meetings. Now, I may have been practicing my penmanship, taking a nap or even eating a snack, but I was incubated in prayer the entire time.

Prayer was not only the foundation of our church but it was a staple in our home. My parents lived by the scripture in *Joshua 24:15, "As for me and my house we will serve the Lord."* Being committed to our church was my

❧

I want to encourage all parents to take every advantage to expose your children to the presence of God. They may not be aware of their surroundings, but I am proof positive that spiritual seeds can be planted at a very early age.

❧

only option. For as long as I can remember, I have loved Jesus, and have always found the power of God to be very intriguing. I was baptized at the age of seven by Rev. Dr. Benjamin Garrett, however, I did not receive the gift of the Holy Ghost with the evidence of speaking in tongues until I was 19. Although I had always been around prayer, this is when I fell in love with it.

Prayer has been my hiding place and my refuge. It's where I am most comfortable because it ushers me into the presence of God. I love the way it feels. There is no judgement or chaos there; only acceptance, infinite love, and perfect peace. *Psalm 16:11 states that, "…In thy presence is fullness of joy, at thy right hand are pleasures for evermore."* While Philippians 4:6 tells us to make our request known to God, I must admit, that is seldom the reason why I enter my proverbial prayer closet. My reason for prayer is to experience his presence.

I am so grateful for the blood of Jesus that opened our window of communication with God. Can you imagine what our lives would be like if we could not call on a power that is higher than ourselves? When all else fails in the earth, we can ascend into prayer and tap into infinite wisdom, dunamis power, and the genesis of creativity that is God.

1

My Definition of Prayer

*P*rayer is simply communicating with God. If there is no conversation, there is no prayer. The vehicle to prayer can be his word, worship, supplication, intercession, request, praise or worship. All of these "modes of transportation" will drive you into the presence of God, which is the ultimate destination of prayer.

When you begin your prayer journey, you will usually find yourself striking up the conversation with God. At the beginning you may find this to be somewhat arduous, however, I encourage you to stay the course and maintain your commitment. As you mature in prayer, the tables will begin to turn and periodically, God will initiate the conversation. You may have a thought or hear a song of worship or praise that will lead you into prayer. You may feel God pulling you away to be alone with Him and that will lead you into prayer. During your bible study a certain scripture may come alive to you and that may lead you into prayer. It doesn't matter which vehicle you use, as long as you arrive at the destination of His presence.

2

It's Just A Conversation

*I*n the book of Luke, chapter 11, the disciples asked Jesus to teach them how to pray. This is how Jesus answered them, "When you pray, say..." Prayer is a conversation, that's it; a conversation with God.

The best conversations are the ones without interruption or third parties. When you have a private conversation with someone you trust, you can freely and genuinely express yourself without judgement. God wants us to come to Him just as we are. You should never feel intimidated or pressed to pray like someone else. The most powerful prayer is a sincere prayer. For example, if you called your parent, and started speaking like one of your siblings, it would indicate to them that you were insecure in speaking to them as yourself. God wants to hear from you, as you. He doesn't want you to mimic someone else.

We may be impressed by the way someone else prays, however, God is not. The only thing that impresses God is the conversation that he has with you, the real and authentic you. The one that he created. God wants to hear the voice that is connected to your heart.

In the 16th chapter of 1 Samuel, we find the story of Samuel going to Jesse's house to find the next king. In the 7th verse, God told Him not to choose a king from the outward appearance. This is because that is not what God looks at; he looks at your heart. You must always pray from the position of your heart. Speak like yourself. God understands slang, split vowels, conjugated verbs, and anything else that you may feel is unacceptable or improper. He understands it all and loves hearing any communication that comes from his children. Now, Jesse's other sons looked the part, but David had a heart for God and was anointed the next king of Israel.

When I visit my parents, I can see their countenance lift as I walk through the door. There are smiles on their faces and they are happy to see me; our Father God feels the same way. He is always happy to hear from you. If you want to put a smile on God's face, stop by and pay Him a visit in prayer. He would love to hear from you.

3

God Wants Your Attention

*P*arents, I am sure that you have experienced times when your child wanted your attention. If they are not receiving enough of it, they will do something out of the ordinary to get it. When life hits us with situations that are out of the ordinary, it can shake our foundation, and bring us to our knees to recalibrate our focus and attention back to God.

On September 11, 2001, the United States was attacked by terrorists. Their targets were the World Trade Center, also known as the "Twin Towers" in New York, the Pentagon in Virginia, and the White House in Washington DC. Most everyone remembers exactly where they were when they received the news of the attack. They remember the devastation, grief, hopelessness and anger that they felt. It's reported that 2,996 people were killed, and more than 6,000 people were injured.

According to Fox News, on September 16th, the following Sunday, roughly half of the adult population in the United States attended a religious service. A few months later, by November, the attendance was back to normal. Typically, when God rescues us from a desperate situation, we often retreat to our previous place of spiritual comfort and complacency.

I have often heard people say that when devastation happens in one's life, God is trying to get their attention.

God will never have to get your attention if he already has it.

There is a song in the movie, *The Color Purple* entitled, *"God is trying to tell you something."* Although I appreciate the performance and lyrical content of the song, it often reminds me to never be in a place where God is trying to get my attention. We should make every effort to stay in constant communion with God. If we always pray like we're in the fire, the fiery flames of tribulation will not have to ignite our prayer lives. If we pray daily without an urgent request, when an emergency arises, it will only necessitate a slight mention during our regularly scheduled prayer time.

4

Prayer Spaces

*J*n Matthew 26:36, Jesus went with His disciples to a place called Gethsemane, and he said to them, *"Sit here while I go over there and pray."* In order to grow in prayer, you must discipline yourself to spend time alone with God. When I question people about their prayer time, some will say, "I pray while I'm driving." Others have told me, "I pray at work" or "while I'm riding on public transportation." You will never have true intimacy with God if you don't spend uninterrupted time alone with Him.

As you begin to seek a deeper level in prayer, I encourage you to designate a space where you are free to go every day. In biblical times, prayer was a religious ritual that could only take place in a temple. 1 Corinthians 6:15 tells us that our bodies are the "Temple of the Holy Ghost." This means that the Holy Ghost can dwell within your body which is your temple. Jesus' sacrifice on the cross allows us the freedom to pray wherever and whenever we want. You've been granted access to pray freely. Locate a specific space and make a reservation for two; you and God.

There is something very special about meeting God daily in a designated area. Over time, you will find that space becomes hallowed and holy. Prayer will become easier and entering into the deeper presence of God will take less time.

I was mentoring a mother of five on prayer. Finding time alone with God was a struggle for her. She trained her children not to interrupt her when she was in the bathroom. So, I encouraged her to make the bathroom her designated space to meet God. This worked out very well for her. Her bathtub became her altar as she knelt there to pray, uninterrupted by her children.

My designated prayer space is in front of my fireplace in my home. I'm not fond of winter but I love praying in front of my burning fireplace in the colder months. Hebrews 12:29 refers to God as being a consuming fire; perhaps this supports my love for it. The summer is my favorite season and I enjoy praying near large bodies of water. I even choose to vacation near oceans, seas and lakes for this very reason. Genesis 1:2 confirms that the Spirit of God moved upon the face of the water. I encourage you to pray near the ocean, seaside, or near a lake; there is something very special about it. You will feel so close to God as his presence envelopes you in nature. Please, let me know how this works for you.

5

Onederful Prayer Meeting

*I*t was approximately 9 a.m. on a Saturday morning when the Lord whispered in my ear, "Call my daughters back to the altar to me in prayer." At that very moment, the seed of Onederful Prayer was conceived. The first meeting was on February 2, 2011. Presently the meeting is held on the same day and at the same time of its conception on the first Saturday of every month.

The concept of the name "Onederful Prayer" is to have a wonderful prayer experience by spending one-on-one time with God. Although it is a corporate prayer meeting, the focus is on teaching and training women to have an intimate experience with God while among others. The success of corporate prayer is the personal prayer contribution that every individual makes.

The first few meetings were held at the Sax Hotel in the "Chicago Loop." It was marketed as a "lunch break" prayer gathering for corporate women who needed help dealing with the pressure and stress of corporate America. Once I completed this assignment, I needed to find an affordable space to rent on the South side of Chicago.

A dear friend of mine taught me how to think "outside the box." He shared with me the story of a minister who had a bible study in a coffee house. Once the coffee house closed, bible study would take place and the attendees would continue to patronize the business. Needless to say, both parties were blessed. I took this same approach with Triniere Poole, the owner of a local Chicago boutique called *Haute Pink*. I pitched my idea to have my prayer meeting in the store before it opened and she graciously welcomed the opportunity. We prayed in the middle of shoes, handbags, clothes and accessories. After prayer, the onederwomen patronized the business. It was a great partnership and equally beneficial.

If you are starting a ministry, please know that God has called you into ministry and not into debt. Where God guides he provides. Start where you are, work with what you have, and adhere to your budget.

God's hand was upon Onederful Prayer. Our numbers doubled after 7 meetings at the boutique. In October of that same year, we moved to a larger facility, *The Connection*. By the grace and favor of God, our numbers doubled again. The Lord made room for us to move to our present location, *The New Zion Upper Room Banquet Hall*, located in the heart of Chicago.

Onederful Prayer is a compilation of worship, prayer, and the word, that is not supported by one specific church or denomination. If you believe in praying to God in the name of Jesus, and the power and presence of the Holy Spirit, you are welcome. The testimonies of healing, deliverance, restoration and financial breakthrough are innumerable. Women come from far and near to have the Onederful Prayer experience.

6

The Prayer of Worship

salm 132:7-8, "Let us go to his dwelling place, let us worship at his footstool, saying Arise, Lord, and go to your resting place...." When we worship God in prayer, we ascend to where he is; God is too holy to condescend to our level.

The Hebrew word for worship is "Shahhah" and the Greek word is "Latreia." They both mean to bow, lay prostrate or kneel. Webster's definition of worship is, "reverence offered to a divine being or supernatural power." My definition of worship is simply telling God who he is. You're probably saying to yourself, "Doesn't he already know?" Yes, he does. When we declare specific attributes of God, it fuels our faith which causes Him to flex and show Himself strong in that area.

∾

Transparent Moment: Sometimes, during my prayer time, I would just read Psalms aloud and weep before the Lord in worship. The word of God can be your "worship leader."

∾

In order to worship God effectively, we must first know who he is. We gain this knowledge by studying his word. I recommend reading the book of Psalms; it's a great way to increase your knowledge of God.

If you still find yourself struggling with what to say, try using the alphabet to give you a jump start. For example, God you are…

- **A**wesome

- **B**eautiful

- A **C**onqueror

- **D**ivine

- **E**verlasting

- **F**aithful

- **G**reat

- **H**oly

- **I**ndescribable

- **J**ust

- **K**ing of Kings

- **L**ord of Lords

- **M**ighty

- **N**obody Like You

- **O**mnipotent

- **P**owerful

- **Q**uick

- **R**ighteous

- My **S**avior

- **T**riumphant

- **U**ndefeated

- **V**ictorious

- **W**hatever I need you to be

- **Y**ahweh

After using the alphabet as a jumpstart, you will feel yourself warming up in worship. Now, let's turn it up a notch and make it personal. A verbal expression of love and appreciation is declared frequently in a healthy relationship and the same is true with God. Think of who God is to you personally and begin to verbally express that. This is the affectionate part of worship. God is great, mighty and powerful, but he is also affectionate. By nature, I am a very affectionate person, and you may have already guessed that this is my favorite type of prayer.

One of my favorite characters in the bible is David. David is said to have written approximately 73 of the 150 Psalms. He is described as "a man after God's own heart."

I believe that this description does not only mean that David had a special place in God's heart, but that David was after God's heart, chasing and pursuing Him in every way. David would worship so vehemently, it left God no other choice than to be captured by David as he worshipped Him. The goal of every Christian should be to worship God in such a radical way that invites Him to dwell with us.

7

The Prayer of Request

*P*eople often ask me, "How do I get my prayers answered?" First, you have to ask. I was well loved as a child. I could've easily been a spoiled brat because I was the baby of the family, but I made a conscious effort not to be that way. I worked hard to gain my independence at an early age. I remember having a conversation with my mother about something that I wanted and she said to me, "Your daddy will give you anything that you want, all you have to do is ask him." She was referring to my natural father and I offer you this same truth of your spiritual Father God. All you have to do is ask Him." *Mark 11:24 says, "Therefore I tell you whatever you ask for in prayer, believe that you have received it and you shall have it."*

Whatever You Ask

There are those who have intercessors on speed dial whenever they need divine intervention. Instead of praying themselves, they solicit the prayers of others who they are confident that God hears. Unfortunately, they are not fully convinced that they have the same privilege of communication. To pray effectively, you must be confident that God hears you. 1 Peter 3:12 says, *"For the eyes of the Lord are on the righteous and his ears are attentive to their prayer..."*

Believe that You Have Received

Before you end your prayer of request, visualize having your request in your possession. If you're praying for healing, see yourself healed. If you're praying for a loved one to be born again, see them worshiping God next to you in church. If you're praying for a new home, see yourself in your new home. Begin to thank God for every furnished room that is specific to your taste. Walk through it and look at it.

∼

You shall have it when you believe that you have already received it, that is when it becomes yours.

∼

John 14:13, "And I will do whatever you ask in my name..."

There was a very popular stage play in Chicago. The tickets were sold out immediately. Although it was sold out, there are always a few seats left for the cast members. I knew the producer of the play, so I asked Him to do me a favor and give two of my friends a pair of tickets. He said to me, "Tell them to go to 'Will Call' and give the ticket agent your name." Because of my name, they received access to the play they desired to see. It's the same with the name of Jesus. The name of Jesus will open doors, give us favor and grant us access to the things that we desire. This is not a myth. Jesus Himself said, "If you ask anything in my name, I will do it." So, confidently make your request and seal the deal with the name of Jesus.

8

Pray The Word

The bible is the written word of God. To pray effectively, you must have a conversation with God using his word. Everything that God wants you to know about Him, and every answer to life's questions can be found in the bible. You must be fully convinced of the integrity and truth of God's word when you use it to pray. *Numbers 23:19 says, "God is not a man, that He should lie, or a son of man, that He should change His mind. Does He speak and not act? Does He promise and not fulfill?"*

When you pray the word, you are literally telling God what he promised you and he has to fulfill his promise. In Isaiah 43:26 God says, *"Put me in remembrance: let us plead together: declare thou, that thou mayest be justified."* In this verse, God is encouraging us to remind Him of what he said, so that we can justify our reason for having our prayers answered. When you pray the word, you build your case and a solid foundation to stand on.

When you find yourself in dire straits, you will be tempted to pray from a place of fear and hopelessness. As human beings, it is normal to react this way. When this happens, I encourage you to quickly recover by returning to the word of God. Search your bible's concordance or simply google scriptures concerning the specific situation that you're faced with. After you locate them, your faith will begin to rise as you speak and declare those scriptures aloud as a remedy for the issue.

Romans 10:17 says, "So then faith comes by hearing, and hearing by the word of God."

There is a metamorphosis that happens in your soul as you hear God's word; your doubt turns into faith. It becomes more powerful as you hear yourself speak it. Before we move forward, take note of the following examples:

Healing:

Father, I am reminding you that you said in Isaiah 53:5 that I am healed by your stripes. Your word proves that I have a right to receive it. I receive healing now in the name of Jesus.

Needs:

Father, I am reminding you that you said in Philippians 4:19 that you would supply all of my need according to your riches in glory by Christ Jesus. Your word proves that I have a right to receive it. My need is met now in the name of Jesus.

Household Salvation:

Father, I am reminding you that you said in Acts 16:31 that if I believe on the Lord Jesus, I would be saved, and my household would be saved. Your word proves that I have a right to it. I claim household salvation now in the name of Jesus.

Whenever you find yourself in need, search the scriptures to find a promise that substantiates your right to receive what you are asking for, and pray the word.

Intimacy:

A relationship will never deepen without intimacy. True intimacy requires time. Each month I teach a bible lesson at Onederful Prayer. I have to spend quality time with God so that I can hear what he wants to say. There was one specific time when I was preparing for the lesson that I will never forget. I was in prayer seeking God for the lesson that he wanted me to teach at Onederful Prayer the following month. I literally stayed home all day, praying, worshipping and studying and I got nothing, zilch, nada. I literally felt myself going into panic mode. As I was preparing for bed, I heard the title of the lesson loud and clear. As I begin to worship and thank God for finally coming through for me, these are the words that I heard Him say, "I just wanted to spend the whole day with you."

God's love for us is beyond our comprehension. He is pleased when we spend quality time with Him. When you truly love someone, there are times when you want them all to yourself. During these intimate times you can have an open dialogue, be fully present, and leave the experience satisfied. I encourage you not to rush your time with the Lord.

Be patient in prayer, be patient with yourself and be patient with God.

Remain in your prayer space until you hear something or feel something. Wait on the Lord.

9

Discipline

very successful person has mastered the area of discipline. They stayed the course until they pushed through to another level. You can't be moved by your feelings, you must only be moved by your commitment. Discipline is the key to increasing your prayer life. As you begin your prayer journey, please keep in mind that it is about showing up, and making an effort to pray every day.

There are some days that you won't feel like it, but you still need to show up. If you miss a prayer appointment, be sure to make the next one. Don't beat yourself up, making an effort to meet with God is never in vain. It is imperative that you don't allow too much time to pass between your prayer appointments. For example, when you miss too many days at the gym, once you return, your workout is more difficult, and it is the same way in prayer. If you haven't prayed for a while, when you do, it is more difficult to enter into His presence.

There is a process in physical fitness that is defined as muscle memory. When muscles have been lying dormant for a short time, once you exercise, they will quickly return to their previous condition of strength. You can't allow too much time to pass because you will start to lose the muscle that you worked so hard to build. This principle is true as it relates to prayer as well. If you miss a few prayer appointments, keep those intervals short so that you can quickly recover and regain your momentum.

There is no stagnation in your prayer journey. You are either progressing or regressing.

God looks at your sacrifice and you will never leave His presence without a reward. You may not see the benefits at that moment, but trust me, you are being rewarded in immeasurable ways.

This is what I love about the grace of God, you always have another chance.

You can't be moved by your feelings, you must only be moved by your commitment.

10

30 Minute /30 Day Challenge

*T*here are life, athletic, wellness and financial coaches; I am a prayer coach. Sometimes, a person needs accountability and encouragement to give them a jump-start in prayer and that is what I do.

My coaching skills are never solicited, it is a divine assignment. As I am writing to you at this moment, I am literally in joyful tears because YOU are now a part of my team. God has something huge, life changing and beautiful in store for you.

It is time for the Body of Christ to mature. In my opinion, the Five-Fold Ministry Gifts (Apostles, Prophets, Evangelists, Pastors, and Teachers) listed in Ephesians 4:11

have become crutches for the church and they were never meant to be. There are many things that the Bride of Christ can do on her own. Due to the lack of spiritual discipline, we exhaust and overexert the Five-Fold Ministry. This is why I encourage people to spend time in the presence of God. Anyone can do it. *In Luke 18:1, Jesus tells us that "men ought always to pray."* The Greek word for men in this verse is anthropos which refers to the human race. Everyone must pray.

Before the internet, the post office was my avenue to connect with people and encourage them to spend time with God. I would mail prayer and bible study assignments to my loved ones with an RSVP card enclosed. As you can imagine, this was not a quick process. I'm grateful for the advancement of technology which catapults my reach and makes my efforts more effective. Now, I would like to challenge you to spend 30 minutes with God for 30 days. These 30 minutes will change your life if you commit to them.

Choose An Accountability Partner:

Accountability is extremely important so ask God to show you who your partner is. We must come to the realization that everyone is not willing or ready to do the work to be closer to God. More often than not, your spouse, BFF or family member may not want to partner with you.

Don't take offense, the partner that God has for you may surprise you. Your accountability partner may be someone that you are not emotionally tied to, but will share your desire to be closer to God. Be open to God's choice.

Set a Specific Time To Meet God for 30 Days:

The early morning stillness helps you enter God's presence quickly and effortlessly, it is the optimal time for prayer. Have you ever noticed that when you wake up late and hit the floor running, your entire day seems rushed and off kilter? That is because the energy that started your day followed you throughout the day. When you start your day in the presence of God, His peace will continue to follow you.

Execution:

You are literally going to have a 30 minute church service, on your own, for 30 days. Set your clock in three 10 minute intervals that will total 30 minutes. You will cover 3 areas: worship, prayer request, and bible study. Focus on one area for 10 minutes and then move forward to the next area. Keep in mind, this structure is only a regiment offered to keep you focused in the beginning. As you mature, this will not be necessary. You will learn to flow with the Holy Spirit as he leads you in prayer, but for now, please follow these instructions.

1. *Worship for 10 minutes*

Always start with worship. Remember you are building your relationship with God. Worship is the way that we greet God. We should never greet Him begging for things. How would you feel as a parent, if your children only visited you when they wanted something or didn't greet you with a hello, a hug, or a kiss when they entered your home? Genesis 5:1 tells us that we are made in God's image and likeness. We are like God. The way that you answered the previous question, is the same way that God feels.

The easiest and quickest way to enter into worship is with music. Music has a powerful way of shifting your mood to your desired destination. Your goal in worship is to be ushered into the presence of God, and the right worship song will take you there. There are certain songs that specifically push you into worship and praise. Whenever you hear a song that leads you into worship quickly, add it to your playlist. Play your worship song selections for 10 minutes. Sing, worship, and praise God. This is how you enter into His presence.

2. *Prayer Request for 10 Minutes*

Now that you've entered in, you can ask God for whatever you want for 10 minutes. Ask Ask Ask! You never worry God or get on his nerves, ask Him. There is nothing too great or small. Comprise a list of prayer requests to remind you of what to ask for. If someone asks you to pray for them, add their request to your list as well. James 4:2 tells us that we have not, because we ask not. I want you to pause and really think about this; have you sincerely asked God for what you want? There are certain things that will only come to you through one intercessor and his name is Jesus. Jesus said in John 16:24, *"Until now you have not asked for anything in my name. Ask and you will receive, and your joy will be complete."*

3. Bible Study for 10 minutes

Now that you have entered into the presence of God with worship, and have made your request known, it is time to read the bible. There are so many distractions that will cause you to pull away from personal bible study, but everything that you need to survive is there. There is comfort, wisdom, and deliverance in the bible. Reading one verse can set you free from years of bondage. The bible is a life force filled with wisdom and prosperity.

As you grow, the presence of Jesus will almost feel tangible as you read. According to John 1:14, *"And the word became flesh and dwelt among us, (and we behold his glory, the glory as of the only begotten of the Father,) full of grace and truth."* You can't separate the two. The more word you have, the more Jesus you have.

In John 6:35 Jesus said, I am the "Bread of Life." In John 4:14 Jesus refers to himself as "Living Water." The word (Jesus) is your spiritual food and drink. Eating and drinking once per week at church, or twice per week (if you add a mid-week bible study,) is not sufficient spiritual sustenance. Just imagine if you only ate and drank water twice per week. You would become malnourished, dehydrated and would eventually die. To avoid this, you must spiritually eat and drink daily by reading the Word of God.

If you are undecided on how to start your 10 minutes of bible study, I suggest that you start with the book of Proverbs. There are so many practical life lessons there, I promise, you will love it. There are 31 chapters, so you will read 2 chapters on your 30th day. You will also find that reading this book is very helpful as it keeps you on schedule.

4. Check-In Daily

Each day after you have completed your assignment, check in with your accountability partner. A simple text or email is fine. I encourage you to do something together to celebrate once you complete your 30-day challenge. This process is simple but not easy, if it was, everyone would do it. On day 31, and every day for the rest of your life, you should be able to continue spending at least 30 minutes a day with God without accountability. These 30 days challenged you to start, but you will not finish until your see Jesus face to face.

If I never meet you in this life time, I pray that when I meet you in heaven, we can discuss how my book helped you victoriously navigate through your life on earth by using the power of prayer.

~ Hidden In Him,
Angela

About The Author

Angela L. Martin's media career at Crawford Broadcasting, Clear Channel and iHeart Media spans 18 years of sharing love, joy, inspiration, information, entertainment, and ministry to millions of people around the world. Her media repertoire includes:

106.3 WYBA — Host of *Sky High Praise,*

Gospel 1390 — Co-host of *Gospel Morning Show* with Richard Steel

Inspiration 1390 — Co-host of *The Morning Praise Party* with Lonnie Hunter and John Hannah

WVAZ 102.7 — Traffic Announcer, *Tom Joyner Morning Show*

Inspiration 1390 — Co-host of *The John Hannah Morning Show*

Inspiration 1390 — Host of *Angela and You For Two*

Inspiration 1390 — Host of *Angela and Mark in the A.M.*

In the midst of her media career, Angela's love for prayer and compassion for women impressed her to form Onederful Prayer in 2011. In 2015, Angela received the coveted "Stellar Award" for *Gospel Announcer of the Year* and the "Echoes of Excellence Award" in Media and Journalism from Delta Sigma Theta Sorority, Inc. In 2016, Angela retired from radio and solely focused on Onederful Prayer and Angela Martin Ministries, Inc.

Onederful Prayer convenes every first Saturday of the month in the heart of Chicago IL. It's designed to train women to have a personal dialogue with our Father God in, Jesus' name. Women of all ages, ethnicities, and denominations gather every month for the Onederful Prayer experience. The countless testimonies that come from the monthly meeting are spirit-filled and miraculous. If you're ever in the Chicagoland area on a first Saturday, please join us! Visit www.onederfulprayer.com for details.

Angela's prayer to God is that she will always be found in the center of His perfect will by being in the right place, at the right time, doing the right things, with the right people.

CPSIA information can be obtained
at www.ICGtesting.com
Printed in the USA
LVHW050900150419
614196LV00015B/424